a strongly
held or strongly
affirmed
# CREDO

KNOW YOUR STORY

CONFIRM YOUR FAITH

LIVE YOUR COMMITMENT

## Confirmation Guide for Parents, Mentors, and Adult Leaders

MaryJane Pierce Norton

## EDITORIAL AND DESIGN TEAM

**Andrea Roth Murdock**    Development Editor
**Josh Tinley**    Development Editor
**Sheila K. Hewitt**    Production Editing Supervisor
**Keely Moore**    Design Manager

## ADMINISTRATIVE STAFF

**Neil M. Alexander**    Publisher
**Marjorie M. Pon**    Editor, Church School Publications

# Contents

# Introduction:
# A Book for You

Congratulations. You are either a parent of a young person who is participating in confirmation classes; or you are an adult who has been asked to walk with a young person by participating in confirmation as a mentor or adult leader. And while the young people will be the ones studying the beliefs of the Christian faith and of United Methodists and making decisions about faith, you are an important part of this experience as well.

Without adult support, it is difficult for a preteen or teen to be present for confirmation classes, to spend the time needed to complete assignments, to feel bold enough to talk with others about faith and the church. Without adult support, this part in a young person's faith journey will feel like a lonely path. Without adult support, a young person going through confirmation may lack courage to ask questions, to try out new ideas, to practice the disciplines of prayer and service.

As you read this guidebook, you will be guided to reflect on the following:

- ❥ the development of preteens and teens;
- ❥ the faith formation of preteens and teens;
- ❥ the role of confirmation in a young person's faith journey;
- ❥ the knowledge and information shared as part of the confirmation experience; and
- ❥ the role of the home in aiding faith formation.

Not only will you be reading information, you will be also be asked to reflect on your own faith journey, write comments about the growth you see in the young person to whom you are relating, and take part in activities that support a young person in confirmation. Use this book as a source of information, as a guide for reflection, and as a tool for practice.

## WHO are THese YOUNG people?

Can you remember looking into the face of a baby soon after birth and wondering: *What will this baby be like? What kind of relationship will I have with this child? As my child, will he or she believe as I do and act as I do? As a church member watching this new baby, will I have an impact on the way this child acts and believes?* As an adult caring for this child, you might have made promissory statements such as: "I will always be part of a nurturing community for you. I will always show you love. I will not ignore you. I will make sure that you have all you need to live life successfully."

Whatever questions you may have had when you became a parent, as that child reaches the teen years, those questions might become:

- Who is this person living in my house?
- Will I ever again be able to communicate with my child, without pulling out the information bit by bit?
- If my mere presence as a parent embarrasses my child, how in the world can I carry on a serious conversation with him or her about faith?

Whatever promises you made as part of the worshiping community in support of children, as those children become teens, those questions might become:

- Why do these young people have to disrupt our worship?
- Will I ever see these young people as contributing members of the congregation?

As adults, we often wonder what exactly what our children and youth are learning.

- Are they old enough or wise enough to understand faith?
- Is confirmation really necessary?
- Isn't it enough to simply provide experiences for children and youth to say yes to Jesus?

## are the preteen or early teen years the best time for confirmation?

Yes. The years of 11, 12, 13, and 14 are a great time for a young person to participate in confirmation classes. Preteens and teens are experiencing the change from childhood to adolescence. It is a time for reflecting on the "what has been" as well as the "what will be." This time of changing from a child into a teen is the best time to ask, "What of my childhood (including my participation in church) do I want to carry with me into my teen years?"

## young people don't seem to be able to think very deeply about any topic. won't that be a problem with confirmation?

Not necessarily. The teen years are the time when the brain is in high gear, developing and refining reasoning abilities. However, many preteens and early teens are still not ready for deep thinking about theological concepts. But they are more ready to reflect on questions of faith and delve deeper than they were just a few years ago. They can begin asking—and finding their own answers to—questions such as, "Who is God?" "Who is Jesus Christ?" "How should I act as a follower of Jesus?"

## i never went through confirmation classes. are they really necessary?

While confirmation classes may not be a required part of a faith journey, they can be a meaningful part of it. Certainly, in The United Methodist Church, we believe that anyone can answer the invitation to Christian discipleship, profess faith in Jesus Christ, and become a member of a congregation, without necessarily participating in proscribed classes. But we do feel that participating with other young people in confirmation; enjoying learning experiences together; meeting with the pastor and other church leaders; and taking part in retreats, field trips, and mission projects allow young people to explore more fully the faith they seek to profess.

# My Commitment as Parent

**Name of the young person:**

(Check all that apply and explain as necessary.)

____ has been baptized.

____ has not been baptized.

____ was not baptized as an infant. The reasons for this are:



____ was baptized as an infant. This is because:



**My hope or dream for my child as he or she participates in confirmation is:**

# My Commitment as Mentor or Adult Leader

**Name of the young person:**

**Years I have known this youth:** _____

**Ways we have built a relationship thus far:**

**If he or she has been baptized, at what age did that occur?** _____

**Why was he or she baptized/not baptized?**

**My hope or dream for the young person I am mentoring and in ministry with as he or she participates in confirmation is:**

# CHAPTER 1

# Who Are These Young People?

So just who are these young people? How are they growing and developing at this stage in their lives?

Before you read further, use the space provided to describe what this young person is like as he or she begins confirmation. If your relationship with the young person is not yet developed, these questions can become a guide to your early conversations.

**❥ If someone were to describe what this young person looks like, he or she would say . . .**

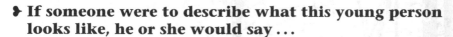

**❥ This young person prefers to spend his or her time . . .**

❧ **This young person says that he or she does/does not enjoy school because . . .**

❧ **I think that this young person would say that our church . . .**

❧ If asked to describe his or her family, this young person would say . . .

❧ At the beginning of this confirmation experience, this young person says that he or she feels . . .

An individual congregation sets the age for confirmation classes. More and more congregations are scheduling confirmation for young people who are seventh grade or older. However, some congregations may have sixth (or even fifth) graders participate in confirmation. That means that young people as young as 10, 11, or 12 may be in confirmation as well as those who are 13 or 14. And as we know, there can also be a wide variety of ages in any one grade. The following information will help you as you consider the weeks, months, or even years ahead with the young people in confirmation.

In our culture, adolescence is the bridge from childhood to adulthood. It might start as early as age 10; and, certainly, with the way maturity has been pushed downward, this can be the case.

The attitudes and commitments made in adolescence help shape the character of young adulthood. This is an important time in a person's journey of growth and development.

Adolescence is a time of rapid physical changes. Parts don't always grow at the same rate; so some youth have big noses, big ears, and big feet. Many of these young persons are embarrassed about their bodies that are growing in these uneven ways.

This is a time of gaining new cognitive skills. Adolescents enter into another phase of rapid brain growth (the first being in infancy and toddlerhood). French psychologist Jean Piaget, long considered the foremost authority on development, spent years developing a theory of how our thinking changes as we mature. Along with Piaget, we once thought that adolescence arrived with the full-blown ability to think abstractly. What more recent studies on brain development teach us is that adolescence brings rapid development in that area, but it is just the beginning of this phase—not completed at this stage of life.

> **The attitudes and commitments made in adolescence help shape the character of young adulthood.**

Adolescents are working to acquire their own values. "My parents think that church is important. My friends think it's boring. Where am I? What do I think?"

While debate continues about the strength of peer pressure on the youth in our society, there is no debate about the importance of peer culture. Ron Tassel calls this "the second family." His argument is that because so many adults are always working, always busy, always on the run, our youth are left to form family support with a second family—their peers. While the youth might not make decisions based on whether their peers will like them, once they make a decision to experiment with sex or drugs or other (often risky) behaviors, their peers surround them to help them with this experience. They behave as family.

> Adolescents are working to acquire their own values.... "Where am I? What do I think?"

## preteens

We refer to 11 or 12 year olds as preteens. It has been said that the 10 to 12 year olds today are going through many of the life experiences that 12 to 14 year olds went through twenty years ago. Certainly, our schools have become more demanding. The sports our children participate in are more competitive. Even physically, our preteens are maturing and entering puberty at an earlier age than we adults did. In our culture, companies aggressively market to preteens because youth of this age have larger sums of discretionary money to spend on items such as clothing, music, games, entertainment.

Many youth receive their first cell phone at this stage in life. And many parents can attest to the unexpected costs related to texting and twittering that reveal a group in constant communication with peers and others who are important in their lives.

Age 11 marks the beginning adolescence, particularly for girls. Behavior you can expect of many preteens includes challenging adult authority. And this confrontation will escalate as they move deeper into the teen years. Saving face is important to 11 year olds. They do not want to be proven wrong or ridiculed. So those funny stories we remember from their childhood become sources of embarrassment, especially when told in the presence of their peers

At age 12, boys and girls alike need enormous amounts of sleep, food, and exercise. Their bodies and brains are growing rapidly.

While 12 year olds do exhibit from time to time great ability to be responsible, the on-again-off-again nature of their responsible behavior at this age makes adults wonder when they can expect the responsible behavior to become the norm. Showing a sense of being responsible is a selective behavior for many 12 year olds. The same young person who shows no sense of care for space at home can be deeply committed to working on a service project for confirmation.

A great need of this age is to be with friends. Girls, in particular, are at the height of forming and belonging to cliques. So if your child's best friends are not a part of the confirmation class, this drive to be among friends might present a challenge for parents, particularly parents of girls. So again, the issue of friends in confirmation can be one that will either delight the 11 or 12 year old or be a source of dismay or discomfort, depending on who else is in the class.

## Early Teens

> **Early teens continue to distance themselves from parents and align themselves with peers, as they seek to define an emerging sense of self.**

We classify those who are 13 or 14 years old as being in the early teen years. Youth of this age are still developing; and indeed, some 13 year olds physically still look like some 11 or 12 year olds. Not only do some still have that elementary-age look, they still have some of the same interests and concerns. Often, however, they seek to hide any of those activities that their peers may see as babyish.

A great word to characterize 13 year olds is *confused*. Many of them are confused about their appearance and about who their friends are. Thirteen year olds can be excited about being a teen and, at the same time, sensitive and tentative.

Most 13 year olds want to talk to their parents but despair about how to start the conversation. Since by now, many of them have retreated to their rooms and insisted on being left alone, parents who also desperately want to talk with their teens despair at not being able to do so. The desire to separate is natural for 13 year olds. So it is important for those of you who are parents to keep having those painfully slow conversations—for your sake and for the sake of your teen.

> Teens ... need forums for thinking and talking.... Having adults who will let them state their opinions ... is very important.

For those of you who are mentors, you may be the most accessible adult for many youth in this age group. Because you are not the parent, you may be able to have deeper conversations with this age group than the parents will be able to have.

By 14, most girls are coming to the end of puberty just when many boys are still in full grip of puberty. The issue of "Who am I?" becomes dominant. Early teens continue to distance themselves from parents and align themselves with peers, as they seek to define an emerging sense of self.

For teens, moral reasoning goes beyond "Will I be punished?" In fact, sometimes their decisions seem to be made in spite of consequences.

Teens are risk takers. Exploring the dangers of the world excites them. They see themselves as indestructible, however, and will take life-threatening risks, without apparent thought to consequences.

For adolescents, self-absorption is taken to new heights: "*my* hair, *my* clothes, *my* needs, *my* wants, *my* schedule." And through all of this, there is often uncertainty. James W. Fowler, Ph.D., author of *Stages of Faith: The Psychology of Human Development and the Quest for Meaning,* sums it up with this verse: "I see you seeing me; I see the me I think you see." However, adolescents might add: "But is that really me?"

Sexuality and sexual encounters cannot be ignored if we truly want to understand the world of teens. To devalue this dimension of the developing self is to close our eyes and our minds to an important part of who teens are as maturing human beings.

Teens need a group to belong to. They wonder, *Which group am I in?* In some school settings, we can still see the delineation of jocks, scholars, nerds, cheerleaders, partyers, thespians, and so forth. However, this is not always easy to see because there is cross over in many of these groups in schools today. However, group is still important.

Teens really do relish adults who will listen to them. They need forums for thinking and talking. Often adults move directly into a "telling mode" with teenagers. Having adults who will let them state their opinions, try out ideas, and question what they see going on around them is very important.

Family can be very confusing for teens. They may be thinking, *I'm not just like them, but I still need them! Am I still a part?*

## THE ADOLESCENT BRAIN IS DOING WHAT?

> **Matters of faith and religion—if not anchored in emotional thought— are less likely to steer behavior later in life.**

We now know much more about brain development and function than we have ever known before. What we have learned affects what we can expect with respect to certain aspects of reasoning behavior, memory, and, emotions. This information helps explain and illustrate behavior of those between the ages of 12 and 16.

What we need to be most aware of in our work and interactions with teens is development of the frontal lobe of the brain. We call the functions of this section of the brain the "executive" functions. This area of the brain directs the capacities of the mind. It cues the use of other mental abilities. And it directs and controls perceptions, thoughts, actions, and, to some degree, emotions. Related to these functions are self regulation, self awareness, self determination and goal-setting. The growth explosion for the front lobe of the brain occurs between the ages of 12 and 16. Until this area is fully developed, adults must do lots of external regulating for young people. This means that parents and mentors are very important in asking the kinds of questions that lead young people to make good decisions. We don't leave them without support, because their brains are not ready for that. We walk alongside, encouraging, pointing out information that might be missed, setting up scenarios to consider.

At the same time that we're considering the frontal lobe of the brain, we can't ignore the limbic system. The limbic system is the site of primal emotions: fear; flight; aggression; fight. And as preteens and teens enter into and are fully engaged in puberty, they are bombarded by surging hormones. These surging hormones cause surging emotions. Thus there are more extremes of emotions expressed, more aggression, and more risk-taking behavior.

As parents and mentors, we want to recognize that emotions can serve the young person well as it relates to learning. In real learning, cognition and emotion are never taken apart. Emotion pushes our minds into needed areas of knowledge. But there needs to be a balance. The goal in learning is to stimulate emotions without always playing them out. Moral and ethical decisions are already made in emotional thought before they get to rational thought. Matters of faith and religion—if not anchored in emotional thought—are less likely to steer behavior later in life.

**As parents and mentors, what do you need to know most in relating to young people out of this brain research?** This age group needs active experiences. Simply talking about the concepts covered in confirmation will not be as meaningful as we might hope. Direct service, talking while working on a project, illustrating through activities will all help young people both learn and express their faith.

How youth feel is as important as how youth think. While the language to express those feelings might not yet be in place, the feelings will indeed be there. Parents and mentors can help youth name their feelings, recognize their feelings, and claim that learning is both feeling and "fact."

## What about Gender?

As we learn more about the brain, we have an increased knowledge about the role gender plays in the ways girls and boys learn. Be clear that there is no difference in *what* girls and boys can learn.

However, there may be big differences in the best way to reach and teach boys and girls.

When talking about paying attention to gender in Sunday school and church settings, we can just about see the questions running through listener's mind: *Isn't that prejudicial? We've worked so hard to bring equality to our boys and girls, doesn't this defeat that equality? Isn't this stereotypical? Are we talking about blue/pink color-coding again?*

> **There is no difference in *what* girls and boys can learn. However, there may be big differences in the best way to reach and teach boys and girls.**

All of those questions are legitimate because we have had a rough time bringing about equality in the way we educate boys and girls, men and women. And the need for this struggle may have not been seen as well through the eyes of the church as it has been seen in public education. It might be helpful to remember some of the past in order to understand the future.

One place to start the discussion is with the question of equality in educational opportunities. By the middle to late '60s, although coeducation was an accepted practice, there remained some vestiges of gender-stereotypical education. For instance, in some schools, it was assumed that all girls would take home economics and all boys would take shop. Even though this wasn't the thrust of any kind of major protest in the '60s, it did indicate some of the gender-based inequities that were still in vogue. It isn't the courses so much but the assumption that it is more appropriate for girls to take home economics than chemistry or unnecessary for a boy to sew.

Many who do not remember separate education for boys and girls do remember the inequity of sports in school programs. Before 1972, a the majority of schools did not offer girls an opportunity to play on sports teams. Girls participated in sports mainly through physical education. But this was the limit. Girls who were talented and determined in athletics rarely found a place to advance their skills and to compete.

The answer to this issue of inequity was Title IX. However, some educators worried about how addressing the needs of girls in athletics might be detrimental to boys. The fear was in some way there would not be enough—enough equipment, enough money, enough personnel to really address the needs of both boys and girls. And so there was fear. There was resistance. There was fight-back. And many, many years spent debating the wisdom of this legislation.

The debate also led to an interesting question. Is providing the same of everything what is necessary? Or are there gender differences that need to be considered in order to create equal opportunities?

The prejudicial view of what boys and girls can or should learn is what we need to leave in the past. And this book stands against such prejudices. However in the years since Title IX, there has been a recognition that same is not equivalent to equal.

Through personal experience with gender specific education and in-depth reading on the pros and cons of such educational systems, we can be more and more convinced that the church is missing out on wonderful faith formation opportunities when we don't plan gender-specific experiences as well as coeducational experiences.

> The church is missing out on wonderful faith formation opportunities when we don't plan gender specific experiences as well as coeducational experiences.

While there may or may not be gender-specific experiences as part of your church's confirmation classes, **here are some things to keep in mind as parents and mentors with young people:**

The way we talk with boys and girls can be perceived either as challenging or comforting, depending on the way we have our talks. Many boys will feel challenged by eye-to-eye conversations. They are more comfortable with shoulder-to-shoulder conversations. Did you ever feel that you got more information from a young man while riding in a car instead of facing one another across a table? That car ride is shoulder-to-shoulder conversation. You may want to conduct conversations about meaningful parts of confirmation as you participate in another activity, such as while

**Who Are These Young People?**

working side by side in a food pantry. Eye-to-eye contact seems to be more comfortable to girls. This implies relationships and more often girls seek first to build a relationship then move into deeper sharing and thoughtful conversation.

Gender differences exist in how we hear. Many boys do not hear the softer voice tones and so will either appear to ignore or disregard instructions. Speaking more loudly and clearly will often elicit better responses. On the other hand, many girls are bothered by loud voices. A girl may experience a voice as being about 10 times louder than how a boy experiences the same voice. Raising your voice with girls can actually inhibit their learning and participation, causing them to retreat from the interaction.

> **For boys, asking for help might be perceived as weakness....While girls might ask for help, they also might be less willing to take a risk or to try a solution on their own.**

Be aware of the differences in how boys and girls form friendship. Boys' friendships are formed usually among 2–12 boys, focus on a shared interested in a game or activity, have as central to the friendship specific activities, aren't often conversation based, and don't include self-revelation. Girls, on the other hand, form friendships based more on a "best friend" or small group of friends, rely heavily on conversation and self-revelation. These friendship patterns show something about preferred ways of relating beyond a "school" experience. A small group sharing time as part of a confirmation class might work well with girls but be only tolerated or disrupted by boys. Turning a learning experience into a game may be preferred by boys and the conversation around the game can then lead to the confirmation topic of the day.

Many times, girls and boys approach asking for help from two different perspectives. For boys, asking for help might be perceived as weakness. Thus they might withdraw from the activity, disrupt the activity, or be frustrated while they try to muddle through without help. While girls might ask for help, they also might be less willing to take a risk or to try a solution on their own.

In addition to knowing something about how preteens and early teens are developing, it helps to know about their generation. All of us are part of a generational group, which is determined by the years when we were born and by life events that happen when we are in our youth and young adult years.

**Particularly important for you, the parent, mentor, or adult leader of a preteen or teen, are these traits:**

**Experience:** This generation is creating a worldview based on experience. This could be both actual and virtual. In exploring faith and truth, life experience becomes their filter. Heart knowledge is important. "Does this touch my soul?" is a question of this generation—even if they don't know how to articulate the question itself.

**Relationships:** As a parent or mentor you may feel young people are obsessed with "screens" - television, videogames, computers, cell phones. But for young people, these screens are ways to connect with others. They seek and appreciate strong relationships with others. When the confirmation experience includes building relationships within the family and within the congregation, it has more meaning for young people.

All of this leads us to ask, "What does faith look like for preteens and teens?"

- **God is with me as friend.** At a time in life when adolescents may feel unsure about themselves, about their friends, and about their family, having God as a steadfast friend is important.
- **I take comfort in what I know, without appearing to do so.** We sometimes call teens "nonconformist conformists." They may have pierced eyebrows, tattoos on their ankles, and spiked hair; but they often still find comfort in the dependability of a familiar worship service.
- **I seek and question.** While not quite ready to declare where they find themselves, they do need the space to ask questions and talk about doubts.

- **Let me tell you what I think I believe.** They seek places to express what they feel and believe.
- **I explore what is meant by *call*.** This is the time when we begin talking with youth about calls to ministry, calls to service. Although confusing, as youth deal with other life issues, they also reflect on what their faith calls them to do and to be. This is true also in the world of school. Many youth are told to have a sense of their desired career by their junior year in high school in order know which colleges to apply to. The church needs to be a part of those conversations too. Call, vocation, and direction—all of these influence and are influenced by the faith of the youth.

## 5O WHAT ARE YOU TO DO?

Whether the young person with whom you are working is a preteen or teen, **it is important for you as parent or mentor to do these things:**

- **Model acceptance and openness.** As you do so, you will be told more about what actually goes on in the world of young people.
- **Talk about feelings.** Help young people define their feelings. Boys and girls of this age know that they have feelings but struggle to know what these feelings mean. Preteens and teens are often unclear about acceptable ways to express feelings. You can provide examples of how to show acceptance, understanding, and caring in socially acceptable ways.
- **Listen often.** Most adults like to talk and have others listen to them. Maybe as adults we've done more talking than listening with young people. Preteens and teens are eager for adults who will listen to them.
- **State your own beliefs.** Even as we listen to our preteens and teens, they need to hear from us what we believe in and how we strive to live as disciples of Jesus Christ.
- **Be prepared for deep emotion and deep convictions.** For many youth, this is the time when something strikes them for the first time as deeply unfair. They are then ready to fight to right these injustices, but they need help in making good decisions and exploring the best ways to make a difference.

As Christians, we seek ways to help us grow in faith. Six denominations, with Search Institute's help, researched the answer to the question, "What makes a church's Christian education program effective?" The denominations included the Evangelical Lutheran Church in America, the Christian Church (Disciples of Christ), the Presbyterian Church (U.S.A), the Southern Baptist Convention, the United Church of Christ, and The United Methodist Church.

As part of the project, the denominations sought first to define mature faith. Their measure was the degree to which persons showed "both a deep, personal relationship to a loving God and a consistent devotion to serving others" (page 9, *Effective Christian Education*). An image to keep in mind that captures that definition is the cross: a vertical dimension of loving God and a horizontal dimension of loving others.

Then they asked the question, "What helps people grow in faith?" From the data came information that looks both at what happens in the formal Christian education program of a church and what happens in the home that nurtures faith.

Through the study, the research team determined that being consistently involved in effective Christian education programs over a long period of time is a key to an individual's growth in faith.

Christian education included Sunday school, Bible studies, confirmation, camping and retreats, youth ministry, and youth groups, to name just a few settings.

Alongside the individual's participation in Christian education, the study also noted the importance of the family's involvement in faith to promote faith maturity. Of the two factors—family religiousness and Christian education—the family was cited as the more important.

> **An image to keep in mind that captures that definition [of mature faith] is the cross: a vertical dimension of loving God and a horizontal dimension of loving others.**

**The experiences in the family that are most tied to faith maturity are:**

❥ the frequency with which an adolescent talked with mother and father about faith;

❥ the frequency of family devotions; and

❥ the "frequency with which parents and children together were involved in efforts, formal or informal, to help other people" (page 38, *Effective Christian Education*).

**Subsequent studies have added to the above list the following:**

❥ the importance of family rituals for nurturing faith in the home. These family rituals include such things as

—lighting a candle at meals to remind one another of the presence of Christ;

—lighting an Advent wreath during the season of Advent;

—praying at meal times;

—offering blessings to one other when leaving or entering the home; and

—special prayers of blessing for the honoree at birthday celebrations.

## FOR PARENTS: OUR FAMILY RELIGIOUSNESS

Using the four points listed above, think about your own home. When do you take the time to talk with one another about faith? When the family drives home after a worship service? When a current event causes the family to struggle together to understand what has happened? When a question of faith is on the mind of a family member? In these conversations young people are often able to link "something I believe" with "something I do."

> Of the two factors—family religiousness and Christian education—the family was cited as the more important.

The structure of family devotions was not defined in the research. Having family devotions could include elements such as a very simple meditation, the reading of a Scripture, and/or prayer together.

Family service projects were not defined either. They were simply classified as projects to help others. Families today have a range of possibilities for helping others.

Consider the four areas: faith conversations as a family, family devotions, family projects to help others, and family rituals. What do you do now? What could you do in your family? Take some time to thoughtfully answer the questions on pages 26–29. Use the questions as a guide for creating or further developing intentional faith habits among your family members.

## TALKING WITH ONE ANOTHER ABOUT FAITH

❯ **When do we talk with one another about faith? When are we most likely to do this?**

❯ **When could our family intentionally plan to talk with one another about faith issues?**

## FAMILY DEVOTIONS

❧ **What kind of devotion schedule would work in our family?**

❧ **What resources might we use for our family devotion?**

## FamiLY prOJECTS TO HeLp OTHerS

➤ **What could we do as a family to help others in our congregation?**

➤ **What could we do as a family to help others in our neighborhood?**

## FaMiLY FaiTH riTuaLS

❧ **When do we (or could we) pray together as a family?**

❧ **What rituals could we practice in our home that would help us build faith?**

## and what about mentors?

These areas of religiousness can also inform your relationship with the young person. Some of these might be part of the one-on-one relationship you develop with the young person. Others will more likely be part of the experiences of the entire group with mentors. It is important to ask yourself and those leading the confirmation experiences about these four areas:

- How will you talk with one another about faith?

- Will there be times during the confirmation experience when worship or devotional time together would be beneficial?

- What helping projects will the confirmation class be engaging in together? Will mentors be included? How will you encourage the young people to reflect on these helping experiences and what they have to say about faith?

- What rituals will be part of the confirmation experience? Will there be times to mark such important experiences as the selection of a mentor; progress made in the confirmation experience, and the conclusion of the experience?

## what about building assets?

Another Search Institute study of students in grades six through twelve also produced important information for adults who work with young people and parents. In analyzing the surveys, Search Institute discovered that the difference between troubled teens and those leading productive and positive lives was the presence of what they called "developmental assets." The determined assets help answer the question, "What can we add to the lives and experiences of young people that will lead them more toward the productive and positive and help guard against those behaviors that are destructive to self and others?" These assets provide guidance to families, as well as congregations in supporting youth.

Assets have a cumulative effect. The more assets young people have, the better the chance for them to lead productive and healthy lives. Conversely, the fewer assets they have the more likely they are to be involved in risk-taking behavior.

Search Institute has identified forty assets for adolescents (ages 12–18). All of them are important and worth finding out more about; visit their website (*www.search-institute.org*) or ask your pastor or youth director to follow up with more information for you. Search Institute provides numerous resources for helping parents, mentors, teachers, and congregations be more aware of and effective in building assets in youth.

Assets are divided into the categories of "external" and "internal." External are part of the environment in which the young person operates. In reading about those related to the community, think of your congregation as part of the community that surrounds each youth. Internal assets are part of the young person's own being.

You might choose to refer to this list as you read through the lessons and opportunities that are part of the confirmation experience. It is hoped that there will be many places where you can see how what is planned reinforces these assets.

Confirmation does lend itself to enriching the lives of young people. It is much more than simply a series of lessons where youth learn about church. The learning is important; so is the experience and the support of adults as the youth participate and begin to make significant decisions.

Of the forty assets for adolescents, the ones listed here align most closely with the confirmation experience.

## EXTERNAL ASSETS

1. **Family Support**—Family life provides high levels of love and support

2. **Positive Family Communication**—Young person and her or his parent(s) communicate positively, and young person is willing to seek advice and counsel from parents.

3. **Other Adult Relationships**—Young person receives support from three or more nonparent adults.

7. **Community Values Youth**—Young person perceives that adults in the community value youth.

8. **Youth as Resources**—Young people are given useful roles in the community.

9. **Service to Others**—Young person serves in the community one hour or more per week.

11. **Family Boundaries**—Family has clear rules and consequences and monitors the young person's whereabouts.

14. **Adult Role Models**—Parent(s) and other adults model positive, responsible behavior.

16. **High Expectations**—Both parent(s) and teachers encourage the young person to do well.

19. **Religious Community**—Young person spends one hour or more per week in activities in a religious institution.

20. **Time at Home**—Young person is out with friends "with nothing special to do" two or fewer nights per week.

## INTERNAL ASSETS

26. **Caring**—Young person places high value on helping other people.

27. **Equality and Social Justice**—Young person places high value on promoting equality and reducing hunger and poverty.

28. **Integrity**—Young person acts on convictions and stands up for his or her beliefs.

29. **Honesty**—Young person "tells the truth even when it is not easy."

30. **Responsibility**—Young person accepts and takes personal responsibility.

31. **Restraint**—Young person believes it is important not to be sexually active or to use alcohol or other drugs.

32. **Planning and Decision Making**—Young person knows how to plan ahead and make choices.

33. **Interpersonal Competence**—Young person has empathy, sensitivity, and friendship skills.

39. **Sense of Purpose**—Young person reports that "my life has a purpose."

# CHAPTER 2

# What Is Confirmation?

You may be asking yourself, *What is confirmation?* If you grew up in The United Methodist Church or another faith community, such as the Lutheran Church, that also practices confirmation, you may be able to answer that question. To start you thinking, here are a few common questions about confirmation:

### Is confirmation the same as bar mitzvah or bat mitzvah in the Jewish tradition?

No. In the Jewish tradition, when a boy or girl reaches the age of 13, he or she is viewed as an adult and, therefore, enters into the community of faith through a ceremony—*Bar Mitzvah* for boys; *Bat Mitzvah* for girls. Confusion comes because these Jewish ceremonies are similar to confirmation. They occur at approximately the same age. They occur after study of the faith. They signify a maturation on the part of children who have been part of the faith community and who are moving into a different life stage. As you read the more detailed explanation of confirmation that follows, notice the particularities of confirmation and the differences between the traditions.

### Is confirmation a time when people are re-baptized?

No. In preparation for being confirmed and as a part of the service of confirmation, if there are those who were baptized at a younger age, the congregation and the one to be confirmed are reminded of the vows taken on their behalf at baptism. Those not yet baptized will be baptized before being confirmed. Baptism, in the United

Methodist tradition, is recognized as God's action of claiming us as children. It is God's action, and it is a once-and-for-all-time action. Look for a further explanation of baptism in this chapter.

## is confirmation something people of any age can do?

Yes. However, in most congregations of The United Methodist Church, confirmation has been a time of intense learning and reflection for preteens and young teens. Some congregations may also provide similar experiences for adults. And these opportunities often prove to be very important for adults coming to the faith with no childhood experiences of the church or those who were previously part of another faith tradition.

Through confirmation, all who participate are invited to learn about and reflect on the basic beliefs of Christianity and the beliefs and policies specific to The United Methodist Church, and to make a decision for professing faith in Jesus Christ. Then they confirm that decision in front of the congregation. The experiences of both the learning and the ritual are powerful for any person coming to faith.

## is confirmation something a preteen or teen can do who has not grown up in the church or has not been baptized?

Yes. Perhaps a family was not part of a church when their children were younger. Or perhaps a family has been a part of a church but was inactive until its children reach the age of confirmation. Or perhaps a youth has become interested in church because of friends. Congregations generally invite all young people of a certain age to be a part of the confirmation experience. And while this range of backgrounds might mean that some concepts of faith are more familiar to some of the participants than to others, it is hoped that all participants will learn new information and expand their faith throughout confirmation. This is an opportunity to carefully go through the concepts of faith and allow time for those in the group to question, to learn, to experience, to challenge one another, and to grow.

## WHEN PEOPLE TALK ABOUT BEING "SAVED" OR BEING "BORN AGAIN" IS THAT THE SAME AS CONFIRMATION?

Not really. Most people use the language of being "saved" or "born again" to refer to a time of recognition of one's own sin and the need for salvation by God.

Often accompanied by deep emotion, the decision to repent or change and become a follower of Christ is inherent in what it means to be saved or born again. Confirmands might mean all of that when they stand before the congregation and profess their faith. But for many United Methodists, the most important image is that of recognizing God's love for us and saying yes to living a life obedient to God's vision for the world.

> For many United Methodists, the most important image is that of recognizing God's love for us and saying yes to living a life obedient to God's vision for the world.

❖❖❖❖❖❖❖❖❖❖❖❖❖

With the above five questions in mind, let's look more fully at confirmation in The United Methodist Church. In order to understand where we are today, we need to have a sense of where we've come through in the years since the start of Christianity. Even for those of us with little interest in church history, these highlights will help us see some of the central questions and beliefs. And whether you are a parent of a confirmand, a mentor, or an adult leader of youth, it is important to be prepared to answer some complex questions that the youth ask. Of course, if the questions go deeper than this short review allows, it's always acceptable to refer the questions to your pastor and other confirmation leaders.

## OUR EARLY CHURCH TRADITIONS

In the early church, baptism and confirmation were one rite. The baptized person was anointed with oil in the sign of the cross on his or her forehead, the bishop laid on hands, and the newly baptized and confirmed person received the Lord's Supper. The imagery and theology of initiation and new birth applied to both aspects of the rite. The liturgical act of baptism and confirmation was complete in itself. Our current United Methodist services of the baptismal covenant encompass these rites. Anointing with oil in the sign of the cross is still possible if it is chosen as part of the ritual. And the laying on of hands after baptism (including infant baptism) is the same movement and purpose as in the early rites of baptism.

Most of those baptized/confirmed in the early church were adults. As a new faith tradition, many were converts, coming to the faith as adults. But we do have accounts of families—including children—being baptized all together and becoming part of the body of believers. In the Book of Acts in the New Testament, we read of all in Lydia's household being baptized and brought into the faith together. And we read about the same thing happening with the Philippian jailer.

> **We do have accounts of families—including children—being baptized all together and becoming part of the body of believers.**

We can also surmise from the writing of early Christians that infants and children were being baptized along with adults. Tertullian, an early church leader, who wrote and taught in Carthage (North Africa) from A.D. 195 to about 225, was an opponent of infant baptism. If infant baptism had not been a practice of the early church, there would have been no reason for Tertullian to write voicing his opposition. And from the writings of both Tertullian and Hippolytus, an early church leader who lived and worked in Rome, we are led to believe that even with infants, baptism/confirmation was one rite—not separated as it is today.

Why is this important? This rite that wrapped baptism and confirmation as we know it today together separated those who were full and participating members of the faith community from those who were not. As part of the service then, as well as today, believers are asked to confess their belief in Jesus Christ and to renounce evil. In the early church, only after baptism/confirmation could the new ones in faith exchange the kiss of peace with others in the church and take part in The Lord's Supper (also called Holy Communion or the Eucharist). Only then were they were fully included in the life and fellowship of the Christian community.

Something else we see in the practices of the early church was a long period of nurturing of those new to the faith in the teachings and meanings of life in faith. Hippolytus writes that the convert was

> Teachings before baptism [in the early church] focused on the meaning of the Lord's Prayer, a bit of the creed, and Christian rules for an ethical life.

taught the meaning of faith both before being baptized and afterward as well. This was at the turn of the first century. The church then moved to a time of nurture lasting through the season of Lent. During Lent those wishing to be baptized met every day with the bishop, being taught, and learning about the implications of becoming a Christian.

From writings of that time, we learn that the teachings before baptism focused on the meaning of the Lord's Prayer, a bit of the creed (the "Rule of Faith," which is very much like the Apostles' Creed), and Christian rules for an ethical life. In the time following baptism, those new to the faith continued to learn the deeper meanings of faith. The learning style probably isn't one that we would want to adopt nowadays. The new in faith listened to catechetical lectures, with such bishops as John Chrysostom and Cyril of Jerusalem. (If you want to read these for yourself, see the "Catechetical Lectures" of Cyril of Jerusalem at *www.newadvent.org/fathers/3101.htm*.)

And why was baptism so very important? (Remember that baptism and confirmation were one and the same at this time.) Early theologians, including Tertullian, believed that, through baptism, we were restored to the full image and likeness of God. This fullness was lost to us with Adam and Eve in the Garden of Eden. But baptism restored us to a state of grace that they had prior to eating from the fruit of the tree of the knowledge of good and evil. You might choose to refresh yourself by rereading the early chapters of Genesis to be reminded of how our faith story tells what happened.

**What Is Confirmation?**

> God is the source of baptism.... There is no need for re-baptism. God works through baptism, so it doesn't matter at what age we are baptized. It is God's action and cannot be undone.

With subsequent generations and subsequent church leaders, things changed. One of the most famous early church leaders was Augustine of Hippo. In the fourth century, he developed a new theology of baptism that placed the emphasis on baptism of infants. He taught that people were born sinful and thus needed to be saved at birth. Augustine advocated baptizing babies as early as eight days old so that they would not be dammed forever if they were to die before being baptized.

Augustine's influence wasn't only for the time when he lived. Many in the church still struggle with the question of original sin and with the meaning of baptism.

Even as Augustine contributed to an ongoing struggle of understanding in the church regarding baptism, it is critical to note that he also contributed to a defining of baptism that is the accepted view of the church today. Augustine taught that God is the source of baptism. For him and for us today, this means that there is no need for re-baptism. God works through baptism, so it doesn't matter at what age we are baptized. It is God's action and cannot be undone.

In the Middle Ages, the Western church (the Roman Catholic Church) separated confirmation from baptism for reasons having to do with the government of the church. Pope Innocent I wrote about this separation when he said, in A.D. 416, that "clearly no one other than the bishop" is allowed to confirm. Only the bishop could lay on hands and anoint with oil, signifying the presence of the Holy Spirit. Parish priests baptized infants, but only bishops had the right to confirm. Because there were long periods of time when bishops were not available to parishes, confirmation was postponed and often done en masse when the bishop came. When the rite was divided, the church came to understand that confirmation somehow completed baptism. Baptism came to be understood as the salvation of the individual, while confirmation was incorporation into the community of faith.

The church next struggled with the question, "At what age may a child be confirmed?" At the Council of Trent in 1556, the question of the age for confirmation was addressed. The first answer was 12; but confirmands had to be at least 7, which was considered the "age of discretion," or the "age of accountability." And once again, a struggle of the early church continues to be a struggle in many congregations, with the age of confirmation fluctuating with different pastors and different practices.

It's important to note that this separation of baptism and confirmation did not occur in the Eastern Church (those we now call Orthodox communities, such as the Greek Orthodox, Russian Orthodox, and Armenian Orthodox Churches). Here the emphasis is still on the unity of initiation. Priests anoint with oil immediately after baptism. A baby is baptized with water, is anointed with oil, and receives the Eucharist all at the same time.

> In the Middle Ages ... baptism came to be understood as the salvation of the individual, while confirmation was the incorporation into the community of faith.

More distinction between baptism and confirmation came as a result of the Reformers, led by Martin Luther, who rejected confirmation as a sacrament. Protestants recognize only two sacraments: Holy Communion and baptism. Both are acts in which Jesus participated. Luther believed that baptism was the sacrament of initiation and was horrified by the idea that confirmation would somehow complete baptism. In fact, he denied that the rite of confirmation was in any way valid. In place of confirmation, he created a catechism that children would learn before they were able to participate in the Lord's Supper. The Reformers emphasized both the sacrament of baptism as initiation and the importance of learning and professing the faith.

Confirmation came to be seen as the work of the person being confirmed, instead of God's work; because the catechism placed an emphasis on knowledge rather than on God's grace, which signified baptism.

Another development of the reformation came from the Anabaptists, who insisted that adult baptism was the sign of a pure church. (*Anabaptism* means "baptize again.") They felt baptism needed to be a deliberate choice and that only an adult could make such choice. So those who were baptized as infants had to be baptized again as adults to be accepted into that community of faith.

**John Wesley ...was a believer in the "one rite" of the early church, where baptism and confirmation were done together.**

Further confusing the matter, another church leader, Ulrich Zwingli, introduced the idea that parents were not to bring in their child for baptism but were, instead, to dedicate their children to God. Dedication served to weaken the sacrament of baptism for infants, since the action swung away from God once more and pointed to human action—that of the parents.

John Wesley did not recommend confirmation to the new church in America, because he didn't think that we needed it. For him, baptism was initiation into the church. He was a believer in the "one rite" of the early church where baptism and confirmation were done together. Methodists would learn the faith in the discipline of the class meeting. All Methodists participated in regular class meetings. There, members were held accountable to and were upheld by one another in acts of devotion, spiritual growth, nurture, and daily living of the Christian faith.

In his book *Claiming the Name: A Theological and Practical Overview,* John Gooch writes about what happened next:

> American Methodism struggled with the theology of initiation for nearly two hundred years, always insisting on infant baptism, but usually as a way to distinguish Methodists from Baptists and Disciples. The 1856 *Discipline of the Methodist Episcopal Church* said that children were to be taught the meaning of their baptism at an early age, encouraged to attend class meetings, and urged to participate in the means

of grace. At an appropriate age, they were to be enrolled as probationers and then later admitted into full membership, on the recommendation of the class leader, an affirmation of the baptismal covenant, and "the usual questions on doctrines and disciplines."

The 1864 General Conference said that the pastor shall organize classes of children ten years old or younger to teach them the meaning of baptism and "the truths of religion necessary to make them wise unto salvation." (from the *Journal of the General Conference, 1864;* pages 202–3. Quoted in *This Gift of Water: The Practice and Theology of Baptism Among Methodists in America,* by Gayle C. Felton; Abingdon Press, 1992; page 105). By 1866, both the northern and the southern branches of American Methodism had a ritual for reception into full membership.

It was not until 1964 that the word *confirmation* appeared in Methodist writings, although there were membership classes before that time. Confirmation is now a fact in The United Methodist Church, having in more recent years become a rite of our church. It is important to consider how confirmation relates to baptism, to the profession of faith, and to a lifelong journey for growing in faith.

## baptism and confirmation

If you were to pick up a copy of *The United Methodist Hymnal* and turn to page 32, you would read what The United Methodist Church believes regarding baptism. This would lead you to the Baptismal Covenants practiced in worship at United Methodist churches. Every one of these covenants state:

> Through the Sacrament of Baptism
>    we are initiated into Christ's holy church.
> We are incorporated into God's might acts of salvation
>    and given new birth through water and the Spirit.
> All this is God's gift, offered to us without price.

("Baptismal Covenant I," *The United Methodist Hymnal,* page 33)

Our liturgy puts us squarely in the tradition of John Wesley. We believe that baptism is the sacrament that claims us as God's own. Confirmation does not complete baptism. Baptism is God's act; it is complete in itself.

> **One becomes a member of the church at baptism....And regardless of age, all are eligible to participate in our other sacrament, Holy Communion.**

The United Methodist Church adopted its current statement of the theology of baptism, entitled, "By Water and the Spirit" at the 1996 General Conference of The United Methodist Church. This statement is carried in the *United Methodist Book of Discipline* and is an official statement of the church. It states that one becomes a member of the church at baptism. It doesn't matter whether a person is 6 weeks old or 60 years old. And regardless of age, all are eligible to participate in our other sacrament, Holy Communion.

Because of our view of baptism, we know this about confirmation:

- ✦ **Confirmation is not a time when one "joins the church."** "By Water and the Spirit" points to confirmation as the "profession of the faith into which we were baptized."
- ✦ **Confirmation can be repeated.** Because it is a reaffirmation of the faith we professed at baptism, it can be repeated throughout our life as we re-embrace our faith again and again as we age and grow.
- ✦ **Confirmation is a rite of sanctification.** John Wesley believed that we are all going on to perfection. We refer to this as "sanctification." This affirms that, as we grow in faith, we are able to become more and more like Jesus, our teacher and example.

So, for United Methodists, confirmation is an act of the Holy Spirit, working in and through the church. The Spirit leads each person to make a profession of faith. The Spirit then empowers each person to live as a faithful disciple of Jesus Christ. For those who have been baptized or who come to reaffirm their faith in Jesus Christ, the covenant states:

> Through confirmation,
>> and through the reaffirmation of our faith,
>> we renew the covenant declared at our baptism,
>> acknowledge what God is doing for us,
>> and affirm our commitment to Christ's holy church.
>
> ("Baptismal Covenant I," *The United Methodist Hymnal,* page 33)

When those who have been baptized come forward to be confirmed, the ritual begins by reminding us of the covenant made at baptism. We are not re-baptized, but we are reminded again of God's claim on us as children of God.

Part of the gift given to United Methodists through the writings of John Wesley is a view of the importance of grace in our lives. It is our belief in God's grace—what Wesley called "prevenient," meaning that it is present in our lives even before we are able to recognize it—that affirms for us God's presence through the Holy Spirit in the lives of our children. It is the Holy Spirit at work in the lives of our children that leads our youth toward faith in God and Jesus Christ.

Confirmation does not impart the gift of the Holy Spirit; the Spirit has already been given and received and is at work in our lives. At confirmation, the pastor leads the congregation in this prayer:

> The Holy Spirit work within you,
> that having been born through water and the Spirit,
> You may live as a faithful disciple of Jesus Christ.
>
> ("Baptismal Covenant I," *The United Methodist Hymnal,* page 37)

It is nearly the same prayer given at baptism. It acknowledges that all of us are surrounded by God's grace and have as friend and encourager the presence of the Holy Spirit. However, the last line in the baptismal prayer commends us to "be" a faithful disciple, whereas at confirmation we are commended to "live as" a faithful disciple. While minute, this change does point out that, at baptism, the commitment is God claiming who we are; whereas, at confirmation, it is the Holy Spirit acting in us to claim our commitment to God and the church in how we live each day.

**What Is Confirmation?**

## SO WHAT IS CONFIRMATION?

- Confirmation is an act of the Holy Spirit.

- Confirmation is a means of grace.

- Through confirmation, we renew the covenant made at our baptism.

- By participating in the confirmation experience and the rite of confirmation, we are further formed in our Christian identity.

- Through confirmation, we focus on our discipleship—becoming a disciple of Jesus Christ by affirming and witnessing to our faith.

- In confirmation, we recognize that we are growing in maturity and in faith.

## GOD'S HOUSE—A WESLEYAN IMAGE OF CONFIRMATION

In "The Principles of a Methodist Further Explained," John Wesley said, "Our main doctrines, which include all the rest, are three— that of repentance, of faith, and of holiness. The first of these we account, as it were, the porch of religion; the next, the door; the third, religion itself" (*The Works of John Wesley, Volume VIII,* Zondervan Publishing House, 1959; page 472).

Think about this as it relates to the three realities of grace. *Prevenient grace* (grace that is present even before we can voice the name of God) leads us to the porch of God's House. *Justifying grace* (grace that is present when we say yes to God) opens the door, invites us in, and makes us a welcome member of the family. Living in the house is a gift of *sanctifying grace* (grace that allows us to grow ever more "perfect"). We have a lifetime for learning how to be at home in God's House and, more important, live in the world a life of witness to God's love and grace.

Consider confirmation as a rite of sanctification that moves us through the door and into the house. We open ourselves more and more to God's love, to God's call to service and ministry in the world, to witnessing to God's gracious acts and the inclusion of all in the family of God. As we move deeper and deeper in our relationship with God, we move deeper and deeper into service, witness, grace and love. And we return to confirmation—as a repeatable rite—to affirm and celebrate our new growth.

## a parent's or mentor's thoughts on baptism

❯ **I believe that baptism is. . . .**

❯ **What I want _____** (*insert name*) **to remember (or be told) most about his or her baptism is . . .**

## confirmation and professions of faith

Confirmation is one of the first significant moments in which the youth affirm the faith into which they were baptized. The youth stand before the congregation and state their own their faith in Jesus Christ. The words are important. The young people affirm the faith—but it is not something they have invented on their own. It is the faith of the church. The ritual begins with the renunciation of all that is evil, the profession of faith, and loyalty to Jesus Christ.

If the youth were baptized as infants, their words were said for them by their parent(s) during that service. The youth now say these words on their own behalf, stating before the congregation that they repent of their sin, will resist evil, and confess Jesus Christ as their savior and promise to serve Christ. If a young person was not baptized as an infant, he or she takes these vows for the first time, stating these beliefs for himself or herself.

God claims us, but we are invited to say yes to God's claim. Professing one's faith in front of the congregation is a time to say yes to God and to claim the name of Christian for oneself.

Faith has a content. In the Baptismal Covenants, the congregation says The Apostles' Creed, which summarizes "the Christian faith as contained in the Scriptures of the Old and New Testaments" ("Baptismal Covenant I," *The United Methodist Hymnal,* page 35). As part of confirmation, the young people will have studied this creed and other church writings that explain the faith of the church. It is assumed in the service of confirmation that the congregation is also knowledgeable about the content of the faith. Therefore, both those being confirmed and the congregation recite this creed, together declaring our faith one with another.

## i bELiEVE

*What beliefs are most important to you? Write in your own words what you believe at this point in your faith journey:*

➤ **I believe that God is . . .**

➤ **I believe that Jesus is . . .**

❥ I believe that the Holy Spirit is . . .

❥ I believe that the church is . . .

❥ I believe that, as a Christian, I will . . .

**What Is Confirmation?**

## A LIFELONG JOURNEY OF FAITH

Confirmation classes are designed, in part, for learning about the Christian faith. *The United Methodist Book of Discipline* (Paragraph 226) mandates that the content of confirmation classes include the following:

1. the meaning of the Christian faith;

2. the history, organization, and teaching of The United Methodist Church;

3. an explanation of the baptismal and membership vows; and

4. a call to commitment to Jesus Christ as Lord and Savior.

But confirmation isn't simply about gathering information and increasing knowledge. It is also about knowing and feeling. It is about standing before believers and saying, "I too believe." It's about standing with believers and practicing the faith in daily living.

The young people are participating in a milestone of faith. It is no small matter to publicly profess faith in Jesus Christ. Many adults find it difficult to stand before others and say, "I believe in Jesus Christ." This is an important part of each person's lifelong journey of faith. It is a time for celebrations at church and at home. It is time to say to each young person, "I'm proud that you have claimed this faith as your own."

We invite our youth to claim the name of Christian and to claim the name of United Methodist. As we do so, we, as sponsors, mentors, and parents, claim those same names. You may find yourself growing more confident in expressing your faith, seeking for ways to serve, and witnessing to the importance of God in your life.

Confirmation is not a graduation from learning. In The United Methodist Church, we have Sunday school classes for persons of all ages because we believe that there is always more to learn about faith. Confirmation cannot possibly answer all of the questions of faith that arise. How we live day by day and year by year is our discipleship journey. It takes participation in worship with a body of believers and in small groups for learning, and support for the rest of our lives.

# My Commitment

*Think about your own commitment to learning. What choices will you make for continued learning beyond assisting this young person in his or her confirmation experience?*

❧ **I commit myself to continued learning by participating in . . .**

❧ **I will continue to support this young person in his or her continued growth beyond confirmation by . . .**

**❖ As a parent, I will support my son or daughter in continuing growth through the following experiences offered in our congregation:**

___ United Methodist Youth Fellowship

___ Sunday school

___ Youth Bible study

___ District and conference youth gatherings

___ Youth DISCIPLE class

___ Covenant Discipleship for Youth

___ Mission trips

___ Other:


**❖ As a mentor, I will support my youth in continuing growth by:**

___ Praying for him or her

___ Taking time to talk with him or her at church gatherings

___ Participating in youth-sponsored experiences for the congregation

___ Engaging in mission and service with youth when invited

# CHAPTER 3

# What Will the Young People Learn in Confirmation?

The confirmation experience, while full of different activities and being designed to immerse young people in a life of discipleship, does have a central goal of providing youth information about the faith, leading them through formation experiences, and opening them to transformation as they make a decision for life-long faith and growth. This may lead you to ask the following question:

**Am I, as a parent or mentor, expected to know all about what the youth are learning so that I can teach as well?**
Certainly, as a parent, a mentor, or another active adult, you are not expected to teach any of the sessions (unless that's your particular role). The team of leaders or your pastor will be teaching the sessions. Instead, your role is to know what content is covered each session, be ready to answer questions posed by the youth, and reflect on your own knowledge and experience as you accompany your youth in his or her confirmation experience. To help you do so, what follows is a very brief summary of what will be covered in each session. With each session is a suggestion of something that you, too, might choose to do to experience some of the content for yourself.

As you can imagine, part of the focus of the sessions is growth. The expectation is that the youth will grow in knowledge and in experience as they move through the content. To illustrate this hope, the youth will be adding to a central image with each session. The image is the vine or the tree. Starting with a simple vine or tree trunk, the youth will add to the image each week as they recall something they have learned from the previous session. They will gradually add branches, leaves, and fruit to the bare vine or trunk. By the end of the experience the image will depict a full range of thoughts, experiences, and information that the youth have recalled.

In addition, each session will conclude with reciting "Wesley's Rule." A benediction helps end a meeting, giving a blessing to all who are present. It also sends the youth out into the world until they gather again. As such, the benediction helps the youth think about what they are called to do as Christians in daily life. You might choose to adopt this same benediction. Write it on a slip of paper to place in your Bible or on your refrigerator to remind you of your call in life.

## Wesley's Rule
**Do all the good you can**
**by all the means you can**
**in all the ways you can**
**in all the places you can**
**to all the people you can**
**as long as ever you can.**

Young people participating in confirmation will be encouraged to keep a journal or diary of their confirmation experience. Some may do this the "old fashioned way"—using paper and pen. The CREDO CONFIRMATION JOURNAL is a good place to start. Others may choose to keep a computer journal if they find writing and reflecting to be easier to do with a keyboard, rather than a pen. The method your youth chooses to use to reflect on his or her experiences is not important. Encourage the youth to take time to think about what he or she is studying and to record reactions—beliefs, questions, or memories, what he or she would like to do because of what has been learned. You may also choose to keep a journal as you accompany your young person in confirmation. This may help you note prayer concerns, list ideas, and record your own reflections.

The content of the confirmation learning is divided into three sections: "Know Your Story," "Confirm Your Faith," and "Live Your Commitment." The first unit, "Know Your Story," includes six sessions that help the youth with information and experiences that focus on the story of the relationship between people and God, as told in Scripture and throughout the story of the church. Next the six sessions in "Confirm Your Faith" move young people into looking at how we express our faith as United Methodists and how the youth can express their faith today. Finally, the sessions in "Live Your Commitment" take the young people through the vows of confirmation, explaining the vows and helping the young people understand what they will be saying and committing to when they are confirmed. Here is the list of all of the sessions:

## KNOW YOUR STORY

**Session 1:** Creation
**Session 2:** Sin
**Session 3:** Redemption
**Session 4:** Holy Spirit
**Session 5:** Church
**Session 6:** New Creation

## CONFIRM YOUR FAITH

**Session 7:** Way of Discipleship
**Session 8:** Way of Salvation
**Session 9:** Wesleyan Quadrilateral
**Session 10:** Worship
**Session 11:** Sacraments
**Session 12:** Living a Holy Life

## LIVE YOUR COMMITMENT

**Session 13:** Renounce, Reject, Repent
**Session 14:** Accept
**Session 15:** Confess
**Session 16:** I Believe
**Session 17:** Prayers, Presence, Gifts, Service, and Witness
**Session 18:** Going Forth

## KNOW YOUR STORY

### SESSION 1: CREATION

You might choose to reacquaint yourself with **Genesis 1** and **2.** The youth will talk about God as Creator and the role of human beings as stewards of the earth. They will also talk about the various names for God. Take some time to think about all of the names you use to refer to God. Make a list of those names on the left side of the space below. Which name has the most meaning for you? Note the name and why this has meaning for you. Talk with the confirmand about what name for God has most meaning for him or her.

❧ **Name for God**　　　　**Why this name has meaning for me**

### Session 2: Sin

A key Scripture for this session is in the **Book of Romans,** in the New Testament. Read **Romans 3:23** and **Romans 5:8.** Often, we don't want to admit that there is sin in the world and that we are all sinners. This session sets forth this part of the human condition for the youth. They will review both individual sin and corporate sin. And through this session, the youth learn that God loves us and forgives us when we confess our sins. An interesting activity for the youth is to identify where they see sin and the need for healing in the world. List below some of the places you see sin in the world. In your time with your confirmand, compare what you identified with what had been identified during the confirmation class session.

❥ **Places Where I See Sin**

### session 3: redemption

You might think of this session as "God provides us with a do-over." In this session, the youth are introduced to Jesus as God the Redeemer. Yes, all human beings are by nature sinners. Yes, we all fall short of the glory of God. Yes, God forgives us. And we have in Jesus the gift to the world of God's son. It is part of our beliefs as United Methodists that Jesus redeems all of human kind through his life, death, and resurrection. An interesting activity in the session helps the confirmands focus on "re-" words, such as *redo, reconnect, recommit, reimage*. What words would you add?

**❯ List of "Re-" Words**

1.

2.

3.

**❯ Choose one of these words and explain how you could use this word to strengthen your faith.**

## KNOW YOUR STORY

### SESSION 4: SPIRIT

Perhaps the hardest to grasp image of God of the Trinity is the Holy Spirit. Reread **Acts 2.** This Scripture helps us see the Holy Spirit as the strength and felt presence of God to enable those who believe to act on their beliefs. In this session, the confirmands will study the images of the Spirit: fire, breath, wind. Each of these—fire, breath, and wind—is a powerful presence. Which of these images of the Holy Spirit helps you best understand this part of God? The confirmands will also look at how the Holy Spirit guided John Wesley, as the founder of the Methodist Movement, and other Christians throughout history. We believe that, with the power of the Holy Spirit—the knowledge that God is with us—we are strengthened to do what we would not be able to do on our own. The stories of these powerful leaders serve to confirm the presence of the Holy Spirit in their lives.

❯ **The image of the Holy Spirit that has the most meaning for me is . . .**

❯ **That image means the most to me because . . .**

## KNOW YOUR STORY

### SESSION 5: CHURCH

You may be familiar with the hymn "I Am the Church." Use the index to find this hymn in *The United Methodist Hymnal*. The words to this hymn remind us that the church isn't a building but people. Confirmands are reminded that, while we might refer to a building as the church, we believe that the church is the community of all believers who together worship God, learn the teachings of Jesus, and practice our faith in service, in our communities, and in the world.

As part of this session, confirmands will review Methodist history. They will also have an opportunity to talk about your congregation's history. See what you can discover about the history of your congregation. What are significant events that you remember as part of your history with this congregation? Be ready to tell the confirmand about one event that shows how your congregation is seeking to worship, teach, and serve in your community.

❧ **Significant events and happenings in the history of our congregation are . . .**

### SESSION 6: NEW CREATION

In this session, the point is made that, through Christ, we are made new. Friends or acquaintances might have asked the youth, "Have you been born again?" Or they might have said, "I'm a born-again Christian." Hearing about being "born again" could cause the youth to question the confirmation process, since confirmation might not feel as dramatic as the implied impact of being "born again."

This session helps young people better understand the term *new creation*. When we say yes to God, it means that we want our life to change or to continue changing so that our actions may match those of Jesus. But the change isn't simply for us personally. When individuals are changed, communities are changed. We transform others through the ways we act out our faith.

Think about an action you took because you are a Christian. What effect did it have beyond you? Use this memory to talk with the youth about how, once an individual becomes new in Christ, a community is made new as well.

> **An example of how my faith has changed my actions is . . .**

### SESSION 7: WAY OF DISCIPLESHIP

Devotion, worship, compassion, justice—symbolizing these four aspects of discipleship is the Jerusalem Cross. We exercise devotion to God through practices such as prayer and meditation that focus our inner life. We join with others to worship God as a public service to God. We care for others by showing compassion and by providing food, shelter, clothing. We address the ills of the world by seeking justice through legislation, protests, and actions that model the character of God.

One suggestion is for the youth to create a personal devotional space. Do you have a space that helps you center your thoughts on God? If not, identify a space where you can focus on God. Place your Bible and a cross or other symbol of faith in this spot. Use this devotional place for your time of prayer and study.

**♪ What spiritual practices do you currently focus on in the areas of devotion, worship, compassion, and justice?**

## CONFIRM YOUR FAITH

### SESSION 8: WAY OF SALVATION

Probably the most defining concept for United Methodists is grace. As United Methodists, we have an understanding of grace that is shaped by John Wesley. Wesley stated three movements of grace: *prevenient, justifying,* and *sanctifying*. This session will help the young people understand each of these movements. You can review the meanings of each of these movements of grace by rereading the second paragraph of "God's House—A Wesleyan Image of Confirmation" (page 46).

In this session, the youth will draw a faith timeline. They will be asked to reflect on their own life and identify times of faith at various ages of their life.

***Draw your faith timeline in the space below. Start with your birth and end with your current age. Identify faith happenings in your life where prevenient, justifying or sanctifying grace was present.***

**Birth**                                                    **My Age Today**

## CONFIRM YOUR FAITH

## session 9: wesleyan quadrilateral

*Wesleyan Quadrilateral:* This is an interesting phrase. It refers to a way of determining whether God is leading our actions. In no writings of John Wesley's do we find him referring to these four ways of judging God's will as the "quadrilateral," but we know that John Wesley relied on all four of these ways of determining God's will.

The first part of the quadrilateral is **Scripture.** What does Scripture say to us, regarding a particular situation or decision? The second part is **tradition.** What do we see from Christian history that guides us? The third part is **experience.** What times in our lives would we call "God moments"? This is our own experience of feeling God with us. The fourth part is **reason.** Does the action we are being led to take make sense? We use all four of these tests to discern God's will or determine a course of action to take.

*Think of a time in your life when you felt led by God's presence. Take time to write in the space below the details of that experience. Then tell your youth about it.*

❥ **A time when I felt God's presence was . . .**

## CONFIRM YOUR FAITH

### SESSION 10: WORSHIP

This session has two distinct but complimentary sections. The first looks at the songs we sing to express our faith. The faith music we sing, listen to, and use in worship expresses deep emotion and beliefs about God. Have you ever gone over and over the words of a hymn or song of faith when you were worried, or joyful, or in trouble? That's the power of faith expressed through music.

The second part of this session looks at worship as a whole. The youth will consider not only what is done in worship but what our worship space says about our beliefs.

*To prepare yourself for talking with a young person about worship, take a look at the following questions and decide what your answers would be:*

**❥ What in our worship space most helps me focus my attention on God?**

**❥ Why does this help me focus my attention on God?**

**❥ Which hymn or song of faith means the most to me?**

**❥ Why does this hymn mean so much to me?**

**What Will the Young People Learn in Confirmation?**

## SESSION 11: SACRAMENTS

In The United Methodist Church, two sacraments are identified: baptism and Holy Communion. Sacraments are rites or practices of the faith ordained by Christ. These are actions that Jesus experienced. They are also open to all. All believers may be baptized. All believers may participate in Communion. Believers are baptized once because this is God's action and there is no need to redo God's affirmation. All are encouraged to receive Communion (also referred to as the *Eucharist, Holy Communion, the Lord's Supper*) as often as we can throughout our life. It would be natural for the youth with whom you are working to be curious about your baptism.

If you have photos from when you were baptized, locate them to show the confirmand. Talk about your memories (and your lack of memories as well) about your baptism. Take time to clarify your beliefs about baptism, and talk with your confirmand about your beliefs.

➤ **In what way are individuals or families in your congregation supported after baptism?**

➤ **What can you do to affirm your commitment to be a part of the journey of faith with them?**

➤ **List any particular memories of taking Communion in a special place or at a critical moment in your life?**

➤ **How did you experience the presence of God in that moment?**

## CONFIRM YOUR FAITH

### SESSION 12: LIVING A HOLY LIFE

This may be the place where many want to stop because living a holy life seems hard and maybe not even much fun. The term used in The United Methodist Church is *Christian perfection*. The youth will learn that Christian perfection is not about being flawless but about striving to have ourselves fully focused on God. A Scripture they will use is **James 5:7-16.** Take time to read this passage as well.

The United Methodist Church has benefitted from Bishop Rueben Job's book *Three Simple Rules: A Wesleyan Way of Living.* Through this book, we are reminded of three rules: 1) Do no harm. 2) Do good. 3) Stay in love with God. The youth will be asked how they might do each of these.

*Identify ways you can follow these rules:*

**1. Do no harm:**

**2. Do good:**

**3. Stay in love with God:**

**What Will the Young People Learn in Confirmation?**

67

## LIVE YOUR COMMITMENT

### SESSION 13: renounce, reject, repent

In this session, the youth will be led through the first of the vows they will take when they are confirmed. They will examine each part of the vow so that they might better understand what is meant by the words of the vow and what they will be promising by reciting them.

The vow begins with "On behalf of the whole church, I ask you: Do you renounce the spiritual forces of wickedness, reject the evil powers of this world, and repent of your sin?" (*The United Methodist Hymnal,* page 34). We begin by taking a vow that acknowledges that there is evil in the world. This statement encompasses both individual and corporate evil. We have "re-" words again. Remember the exercise from Session 3, with words starting with "re-" (page 58)? These words are strong statements about actions we promise at baptism/confirmation.

*Consider what you would name for each of these phrases if you were taking these vows at this time:*

❥ **I renounce . . .**

❥ **I reject . . .**

❥ **I repent . . .**

## LIVE YOUR COMMITMENT

### SESSION 14: ACCEPT

This session addresses the next vow of baptism/confirmation: "Do you accept the freedom and power God gives you to resist evil, injustice, and oppression in whatever forms they present themselves?" (*The United Methodist Hymnal,* page 34). This vow points to the reality that human beings do have the freedom and power to choose. We can choose evil, or we can choose good. If we choose good, the vow lists that we must fight against evil, injustice, and oppression. Where do you see the presence of evil, injustice, and oppression? What can Christians do to fight against these evidences of evil, injustice, and oppression?

**❧ I see evil, injustice, and oppression in the following situations in our community and in the world:**

**❧ I will address these situations with the following actions:**

*(Continued on page 70)*

*(Continued from page 69)*

A large part of the session will guide the youth in considering the freedom they have in making a choice to resist evil, injustice, and oppression.  One of the ways to do so is to establish habits of spiritual formation that enable us to be spiritually centered for making wise decisions. This will also help in making decisions about the actions to take in addressing situations of evil, injustice, and oppression.

The youth will be invited to do the following activity. You may choose to join them in this. Just as an athlete sets a training schedule to stay strong, Christians engage in training sessions of spiritual practices. For one month, commit to doing something every single day, such as morning prayer or reading a daily devotion. In addition, commit to a practice once a week such as attending a mid-week worship service or participating in a weekly Bible study.

**❧ I commit to the daily practice of . . .**

**❧ I commit to the weekly practice of . . .**

## LIVE YOUR COMMITMENT

### SESSION 15: CONFESS

In this session, youth will discuss and experience what is meant by the next vow: "Do you confess Jesus Christ as your Savior, put your whole trust in his grace, and promise to serve him as your Lord, in union with the church which Christ has opened to people of all ages, nations, and races?" (*The United Methodist Hymnal*, page 34).

Two concepts that are emphasized in this session are trust and promises. You may choose to read **Proverbs 3:5-6** about trust and **Ephesians 2:8-10** about promises.

The connectional nature of The United Methodist Church is also discussed. In The United Methodist Church, every congregation is part of a district—a geographical cluster of congregations. The districts are formed into a larger geographical group—the annual conference. And these are part of the global United Methodist Church. A congregation isn't alone but part of a connection. This enables The United Methodist Church to work worldwide. Be prepared to talk with the confirmand about how you have experienced the worldwide nature of The United Methodist Church.

❧ **What do you know about your district and/or annual conference?**

❧ **Have you participated in activities beyond your congregation such as participating in conference events?**

## LIVE YOUR COMMITMENT

### session 16: i believe

As part of the baptism/confirmation vows, persons are asked to affirm their faith through a series of questions that are answered as part of the Apostles' Creed. This is one of the historic creeds of the church. Through a creed, we state what we believe as a church.

As part of this session, your youth will be asked to write his or her own creed (hence, the Latin name *Credo* for this whole program). He or she will do so by looking at the historic creeds and affirming what he or she personally believes at this time in his or her life. If the youth at your church have been using the CREDO CONFIRMATION JOURNAL, they have had the chance to work on the creed throughout their confirmation experience.

It would be appropriate for you to write your own creed as well. Then in meeting with your confirmand, you each can look at what the other has written and discuss similarities and differences. If you are stuck, it may help you to know that many creeds focus on beliefs about God, Jesus, the Holy Spirit, and the Church.

❧ **My Creed (Statement of Belief):**

### session 17: prayers presence, Gift, service, and witness

Up to this point in the service for baptism/confirmation, the vows have been those of the Christian faith. In this session, the vow the youth study is one that is taken regarding your congregation: "As *members* of this congregation, will you faithfully participate in its ministries by your prayers, your presence, your gifts, your service, and your witness?" (*The United Methodist Hymnal*, page 38). Taking the vows of baptism/confirmation doesn't mean simply participating in a ceremony then being done with the responsibilities. It means promising to be active in faith; and it assumes that those taking the vows will do so in light of their individual gifts, graces, and talents.

As part of this session, the youth will participate in a spiritual gifts inventory so that they can begin to name their gifts. Another activity asks them to affirm a gift they see for each other member of the confirmation class.

A statement from you, naming the gifts, graces, and talents you see in this young person, makes a great gift for your confirmand.

***Use the space here to make notes, or write a statement naming the gifts of the youth:***

❧ _____ (*insert name of the youth*) **has these**

   **gifts, graces, and talents:**

## LIVE YOUR COMMITMENT

### SESSION 18: GOING FORTH

This final session focuses on the closing words of the baptism/confirmation service: "The God of all grace, who has called us to eternal glory in Christ, establish you and strengthen you by the power of the Holy Spirit, that you may live in grace and peace" (*The United Methodist Hymnal,* page 39). Notice that it is not a conclusion. It is a blessing for continued life. The concluding phrase leads to the next stage of the confirmand's journey. This part of the journey is to be celebrated, but it doesn't end the journey of faith. The rest of their lives is in front of these young people.

*Because this is a time to reflect on what has been experienced and learned during the confirmation process, it is good for you and the young person to remember together key learnings, important experiences, relationships that have been built. Use the form below to record your thoughts.*

❯ **I learned ...**

❯ **The experiences that have shaped my faith include ...**

❯ **I'm so glad that I was able to build a relationship with**

_____ (*insert the name of the youth*) **because ...**

# CHAPTER 4

# What Is My Role?

Whether you are a parent, a mentor, or adult leader in youth ministry, you become a fellow traveler with youth in the confirmation experience. The experience is not for you, but you are one who accompanies a youth on his or her confirmation journey. What is hoped is that those who accompany youth as parents and mentors are doing so in ways that are safe and that guard the youth. The United Methodist Church takes very seriously the care of youth. Churches have adopted Safe Sanctuary policies to make sure that youth are safe with adults.

Before you began working with youth, your church most likely followed its Safe Sanctuary policies for background testing and setting down expectations. In addition to knowing your congregation's policies, you might be interested in reading more on this topic. The United Methodist Church provides resources for preparing and following a Safe Sanctuaries policy in your church, including *Safe Sanctuaries: Reducing the Risk of Abuse in the Church for Children and Youth,* by Joy Thornburg Melton (Discipleship Resources). The reminders included here are found in that book.

Parents, mentors, and all other adults working with youth need to be aware of safety in the following areas:

> ❥ **Maintain appropriate interpersonal boundaries.**
> Adults set the boundaries, so they need to be clear about what is appropriate and what is not. Joy Melton states that one part of this is always allowing a young person to initiate any hugs and to make sure that the adult is the one to end the hug.

> ❥ **Follow the two-person rule.** This is stated, as follows, on page 85 of *Safe Sanctuaries:* "The two-adult rule requires no

fewer than two adults present at all times during any church-sponsored program, event, or ministry involving youth. For times a mentor meets with a young person, they should be paired with at least one other mentor/young person team."

❥ **Set conditions for cyber safety with youth.** Mentors need to get permission from parents for e-mails, cell phone calls, and texting between the mentor and the young person.

❥ **Expect a written covenant.** As a congregation begins the confirmation experience for youth, many will have a written covenant covering behavior expectations for all involved. This will include the youth, those who are teaching and leading the experience, mentors, and parents. This way, everyone is clear about what will be happening and the codes of behavior.

## Your role as a mentor

> A written covenant ... will include the youth, those who are teaching and leading the experience, mentors, and parents.

You have been asked to mentor a youth in your congregation. Most likely, you were selected because those leading the confirmation experience feel you are a person of mature faith. Depending on what the selection process is in your congregation, you may or may not know the youth you will be mentoring. The following questions have been voiced by others selected to serve as a mentor:

**I don't see myself as that knowledgeable about faith. Why would someone think that I have a mature faith?**
Sometimes we don't see ourselves as others see us. Having mature faith doesn't mean that you don't have questions, doubts, or uncertainties. However, through Sunday school, as part of a DISCIPLE BIBLE STUDY group, or in some other small group, you have probably expressed or shown your faith in Jesus Christ. Being a mentor simply calls upon you to continue doing what you have been doing as one

who seeks to live a life of faith. Mentors function as learners and partners with youth. You aren't being asked to be one of the teaching team; you're being asked to partner with a youth as he or she explores his or her faith. That means that you will most likely be learning as the youth learns and experiencing some of what he or she experiences. Don't think of yourself as an expert in faith. Think of yourself as a co-learner. Be open to being taught by the youth with whom you are paired.

> **Don't think of yourself as an expert in faith. Think of yourself as a co-learner. Be open to being taught by the youth.**

### I don't feel that I really know the youth with whom I am paired. Is that OK?

Some mentors know well the young person they are asked to mentor. They may have taught him or her in Sunday school. They may be a family friend. However, even if this is the case, they might discover that they actually know little about the young person they've been asked to mentor. On the other hand, sometimes the mentor and young person don't know each other at all. Either situation is fine. There will be plenty of experiences planned and activities suggested to help you share your faith and support the young person in his or her faith journey. The focus of the relationship is one of mutual support for faith growth. It isn't necessary to know the person you will mentor before the beginning of the experience.

### The Safe Sanctuary requirements seem as though they could make it difficult for me to meet with the youth I will be mentoring. What do I need to do?

Your congregation might set a schedule of meetings for you to meet with the young person and arrange for you to be with at least one other mentor and young person. If this isn't set up for you, take the initiative to make these arrangements yourself. It's a good idea to set a pattern of meeting from the beginning of the confirmation experience. Expect to have some cancelled meetings when either of the confirmands, the other mentor, or you will not be able to meet. But if a plan is set early, you will have the best chance to maintain regular contact.

**What Is My Role?**

After obtaining permission from the parents, you might find e-mailing and texting to be helpful ways to keep in touch. Posing a short question and chatting through text or online in a social site allows you to have short talks on the confirmation topics. As you might remember, not many youth of these ages are into long discussions anyway!

> **Think of yourself as a partner who is encouraging growth, and so allows for the youth to test out opinions, ideas, and thoughts.**

When you meet with the confirmand, remember whose confirmation experience this is. Because it is the youth's experience, he or she should be getting the larger amount of air time. Refrain from adopting any kind of telling or lecturing style with the confirmand. Practice your listening and prepare questions that will encourage answers beyond a yes or no. The suggestions in Chapter 4 for talking about the sessions will allow the young person to do more sharing than you.

Think of yourself as a partner. But think of yourself as a partner who is encouraging growth and so allows for the youth to test out opinions, ideas, and thoughts. The youth you work with may be more inclined to open up to you than to his or her parent(s). As we claim our own faith, sometimes we reject the beliefs of our parents. A youth may feel afraid of hurting a parent's feelings or making a parent feel rejected. You are a safe adult with whom he or she can test his or her beliefs. This is a wonderful role to play. And as we accompany another on a faith journey, we also explore and test again our own beliefs. Be assured that you, too, will grow through this experience.

## Your role as a parent

You might or might not have participated in an orientation class for parents of those who will take part in confirmation classes. But you may have some questions about your part in this whole confirmation process. Here are some questions voiced by parents whose sons and daughters have been confirmed:

**In my church, each person in confirmation has a mentor in the congregation. How is my role different from the mentor's?**

If your congregation provides an adult mentor for your child, consider yourself lucky. An adult mentor who is not a family member helps connect the young person to the congregation. Having a mentor says to the youth, "More people than just my family care for and support me."

> Youth see themselves ... in the center of a large arena, with the world looking at them....Our job as the church is to populate that arena with faces the youth recognize as caring and supporting.

Youth see themselves as if they were in the center of a large arena, with the world looking at them and watching to see whether they will mess up or succeed. Our job as the church is to populate that arena with faces the youth recognize as caring and supporting. So anytime we can add to the circle of friendly faces in that vast arena, the more support our youth will experience. The mentor does not take the place of the parent. The mentor simply increases the number of friendly faces surrounding your youth.

**How do I get feedback from my child about confirmation? I usually get one-word answers to questions. How will I know what's going on?**

Included here will be some specific questions to ask. Most teens will use the shortest response to any question asked of them. When we ask such questions as, "How was confirmation today?" We're likely to get these responses: "Fine," "Good," or "OK." That's why there are some specific questions posed in this book. However, do remember that this tendency to provide the smallest amount of information possible is not just a characteristic of your son or daughter but one shared by many in this age group.

**What can we do at home? I don't want to repeat what my child is receiving in the classes at church, but I do want to do my part.**

Repetition is good. We learn best those things that are repeated over and over. Do you remember learning multiplication tables? It likely took numerous drills before those number facts were thoroughly embedded in your brain. Home activities that don't center on memorization but on activities that invite discussion, involve everyone in spiritual practices of prayer and meditation, and include family members in service at church and the community serve the same function of repetition as memorizing those number facts.

## My child has one parent who is a believer and one who is not. What do we do in this situation?

Your choice to have your child be part of confirmation shows that you are encouraging your child to explore the Christian faith and decide what his or her response will be to the call to be a disciple of Jesus Christ. In some family situations, the parents are believers in different faiths, members of different Christian denominations, or one is a non-believer. Your child will naturally want to know what each parent has chosen and why. It is important for you to honestly answer any questions your youth poses. And it is important that, as your child enters confirmation classes, both parents agree to allow your child to make his or her own decision about profession of faith and church membership. It is hoped that both parents will also have agreed to support whatever decision your child makes.

## We are busy. I want to do my part, but what about other commitments? With baseball, school, soccer, band, and family commitments, it will be hard to make sure that my child makes all of these confirmation classes.

This might sound trite, but making confirmation a priority could mean that your son or daughter misses some games. Some coaches make absolute statements such as, "No one on this team is allowed to miss any games!" But many others are reasonable about church and family demands. However, don't leave this to your child alone to negotiate. Ask your church for your child's confirmation schedule. Compare this with the Scout, or soccer, or band schedule. See what you can negotiate at the beginning so that participating in confirmation is a priority. Unforeseen factors such as a death in the family or illness can also cause your son or daughter to miss confirmation sessions.

Be clear about ways your child can make up any missed classes or experiences where absences are unavoidable. Certainly, the goal is as much participation as possible. When absences happen, your son or daughter loses out on the interactions, the learning times, and the sharing of faith among peers and with adults.

> This might sound trite, but making confirmation a priority could mean that your son or daughter misses some games.

**What can we do as a family to support our child's confirmation experience?**

Let's look back to those four key points of family religiousness we identified earlier (page 24):

- having conversations with parents about faith;
- practicing regular devotions at home;
- participating as a family in projects to help others; and
- having family rituals of faith.

For practical purposes, this book groups "practicing regular devotions" and "having family rituals of faith" into the category of "Practices of Faith in the Home." Let's look at the three adjusted categories:

## PRacTices of FaiTH in THe HoMe

- **Designate one night each week as Family Night.** Of course, Family Night may be observed more than once a week; but be sure to set a goal of at least once a week through the time your child is in confirmation.

Be intentional about including in Family Night the following:

—eating a meal together;
—spending time talking about a faith issue that has arisen for a family member during the week;
—praying together; and
—playing together by enjoying games, looking through photo albums, watching home videos, making something.

**❧ Practice regular devotions as a family.** Many families use *The Upper Room Daily Devotional* guide. This meditation guide includes Scripture reading, a story of something out of the writer's own experience that applies to that Scripture, a prayer, and a prayer emphasis for the day. The meditations allow all family members to reflect on the Scripture and hear the story at their own level. The discussion can center on what each family member finds meaningful out of the reading.

**❧ Encourage individual Bible and devotional reading.** *Devo'Zine* is a devotional magazine written by teens for teens.

**❧ Establish rituals for devotion and praying.** Many families light a candle, reminding themselves that Christ is the light of the world. Others have a prayer box with slips of paper on which prayer concerns have been written. Daily they draw from the box and intentionally pray for the person, world event, or community need recorded on that drawn slip of paper.

> **As part of Family Night, eat a meal together, spend time talking about a faith issue, pray together, play together.**

Look at the rhythm of prayer in your life, in the life of your teen, and in your family. Prayers at the start of the day, at the end of the day, and at meals are routines that many families find helpful. You may choose to practice some simple sentence prayers for each of these times. Consider these:

**At the beginning of the day:** O God, we thank you for this day that is before us. Be with each of us in all that we say and do today. Amen.

**At the end of the day:** Gracious God, as this day ends, we give you thanks for your love and support that was ours this day. Bless us and keep us through the night. Amen.

**At meals:** Loving God, we give thanks for this food that is before us. Bless those who have prepared it, those who have served it, and those who now receive it. Amen.

Identify and celebrate key Christian holidays as well as other special days throughout the calendar year while your son or daughter is in confirmation. Plan ways to celebrate at home what you also celebrate as part of the congregation in worship. Consider these:

> Identify and celebrate key Christian holidays as well as other special days throughout the calendar year.... Plan ways to celebrate at home what you also celebrate as part of ... worship.

**Start of Confirmation:** Post on your refrigerator, a family bulletin board, or calendar the names of those who will be leading your child in confirmation. Post also the names of the young people who will be participating in confirmation. At least once a week, say out loud the names you have posted, praying that God will guide both teachers and learners. Meet your child's mentor. Share a meal and talk together about your hopes for your child's confirmation experience.

**Advent:** Make an Advent wreath, and light the candles for each Sunday in Advent.

**Christmas:** As a family, make something—bread, cookies, pickles, tea mix—and take it to neighbors, along with your wishes for a blessed Christmas.

**New Year's:** Write resolutions. Without reading what someone else has written, put these in a safe place and set a date of at least two months later to read these together and see what progress each person has made with his or her resolution.

**Epiphany:** Start a tradition of each one in the family giving to every other family member three gifts of time or talents. These might include such things as a coupon for making the bed of another person, a poem written in thanks of a family member, or a coupon for teaching another how to make a favorite recipe.

**Lent:** Ask each family member to give up one unhealthful habit, such as biting fingernails, spending too much time on the computer, eating a lot of sweets. Ask each family member to acquire one healthful habit, such as daily Bible reading, daily exercise, eating at least three servings of vegetables daily. Make a promise to one another to check on progress each week during Lent.

**Easter:** Before or after attending worship as a family, ask each person to say why Easter makes him or her glad.

**Pentecost:** As a family, write notes of thanks to key members of your congregation.

**End of Confirmation:** Ask each family member, as part of family devotions, to place his or her hands on the head of the confirmand and say his or her own prayer of blessing to God for the confirmand.

## TaLK TOGETHEr abOUT FaITH

Make a deck of index cards with questions that you can ask one another about faith. Carry these cards in the car. Each time you are in the car together, have each person in the car select a card and answer the question on the card they have selected. Here are some questions or statements that can be written on the cards:

- What is your earliest memory of God? Tell about it.
- What story from the Bible about Jesus do you most enjoy? Why?
- When have you felt alone and without God? Tell about it.
- Who in your congregation has meant the most to you in your faith journey? Why?
- What sermon do you remember most vividly? Why?
- What place in nature helps you feel closest to God? Why
- What problem facing the world today, do you think, would be the hardest to solve? Why?
- What Old Testament story do you like most? Why?
- What question would you most like to ask God? Why?
- What movie helps you think about God? Why?
- When do you feel closest to God? Why?
- What hymn heard in church means the most to you? Why?

- When have you been involved in helping others? What did you do?
- Think about one of the creeds of the church. What one belief do you have the most difficulty understanding? Why?
- What is something important to you in church? Why?

Each Sunday after worship, ask each family member to say something that he or she will remember from the service.

Add a "What do you think about...?" question for each person in the family to answer as part of your home devotions.

After each confirmation class, ask your son or daughter to finish one or all of these statements:

- The most important thing I learned today in confirmation was...
- I left confirmation today with a question about...
- What I would most like to say to my confirmation leader after today's class is...

Each week, talk with your son or daughter about your faith.

Use the list of topics to be covered in confirmation class (page 55) and think about each topic. Share your thoughts with your son or daughter, then ask him or her to talk about what he or she thinks about the topic as well. Make one of these questions a routine part of your conversation. Be prepared to answer it as well.

- Where did you see God today?
- Where have you seen God at work in the world this week?
- Whom did you spend time with this week who helped you know more about God's love and care?

Talk with your son or daughter about your own faith practices. As parents, we may feel that our youth are aware that we pray daily, use a devotional guide, spend time in silence, listen to and sing hymns and songs of faith, or seek out opportunities of service to others. But this is not always known. Take this opportunity to tell your youth what is important to you for nurturing your faith.

**What Is My Role?**

> **Serve with the congregation.** Ask your pastor or another church leader to give you a list of service projects done by your congregation. Pick one to do as a family during the time your child is in confirmation.

> **Consider neighbors nearby.** Each week during confirmation, do something kind for one neighbor one week and another neighbor another week in your neighborhood or near the church.

> **Make a bank for collecting spare change.** Ask each family member to place into the bank change they have in their pockets or purses at the end of each day. Together decide on a project, and donate the money you collect to that project at the end of confirmation.

> Talk with your son or daughter about your own faith practices.... Take this opportunity to tell your youth what is important to you for nurturing your faith.

> **Serve with the community.** At least once a week, read your community paper with your youth. Look for stories about community service. Pick one or more of these projects, and together think of ways that you and your youth are needed. Examples include collecting food for a local food bank, donating toys (new or like new) to a family shelter, donating clothing, helping with a clean-up day at a nearby school. The project itself matters less than you and your youth doing it together in a way that both of you can participate. That's what partnering with your youth is all about.

# CHAPTER 5

# Whose Decision Is This?

At the end of the journey, a decision faces each confirmand. Will he or she say yes to faith and take the vows of church membership? Or will he or she say, "No, I'm not ready to make a decision at this time"? For those who work with each youth, the hope is that each will profess faith in Jesus Christ and be confirmed in the church. This response isn't always the case. Some questions adults who care for youth have as the confirmation experience comes to an end include the following:

## WHAT IF A YOUTH DECIDES NOT TO BE CONFIRMED?

First of all, as the adults closest to this youth, don't panic. It's important for both parent(s) and mentor to be able to talk with the young person to discover the reason he or she is saying, "No, I don't want to be confirmed." Because not all boys and girls at this age are at the same stage, some may be worried about some things that adults might see as trivial. One may be worried about the offering because she doesn't receive an allowance. Because she cannot say that she would support the church with financial gifts, she believes that she should wait. Parents may offer alternatives and help their daughter with a plan of service to the church that might not involve a financial pledge or regular financial offerings at this time. Another might say no because he feels that he doesn't have the answer to every one of his faith questions. Either the parent(s) or the mentor could talk with the youth focusing on how we all learn throughout our lives. This might provide the assurance he needs to decide to join the church.

However, if the answer is truly no at this time, don't forget that God's grace is still at work. And so should you be "still at work."

Continue conversations about faith, without putting pressure on the youth. It could be valuable for the mentor to stay in contact with the youth, setting up periodic meetings to continue faith talks. As parents continue to do the things you do to express your faith. Invite, encourage, require (as you deem appropriate) your son or daughter's participation in the practices of faith with your family and with the congregation. Continue to uphold him or her in your prayer. And trust God. In the Wesleyan tradition, we recognize prevenient grace—the grace that surrounds us and goes before us—as God's continuing call to come closer. Our God is a God who never gives up but continues to care for each person. That is our model as adults who care for youth.

## Does everyone in the confirmation class automatically join the church?

No. As the classes for confirmation come to an end, each youth will be asked to meet with the pastor and/or church leaders and state his or her own personal decision about professing faith and joining the church. Talk with your young person as the time approaches; find out how he or she is feeling about the conversation and where they are in making a decision. You may discover that he or she has questions that a mentor can answer. Or you may discover that he or she has questions that only a parent can answer. You may discover that the youth have questions that can be addressed in a one-to-one conversation with the pastor or other confirmation leaders. And you may discover, as a youth verbalizes his or her beliefs, that he or she can do so more clearly than you can as an adult.

> **Our God is a God who never gives up but continues to care for each person. That is our model as adults who care for youth.**

Some congregations have a Sunday celebrating the learnings and experiences of those who have been in confirmation but have a different Sunday when the youth actually join the church. This allows those who have participated in the class, regardless of the decision they are making, to be part of a group presenting a litany of beliefs, or creating a banner, or leading in worship. Other congregations do not have a confirmation Sunday but encourage the young people to select a Sunday following the confirmation experience that allows for visiting relatives to attend.

## WHAT IF A PARENT FEELS THAT HIS OR HER YOUTH IS NOT READY TO MAKE A COMMITMENT?

First, parents needs to remember that this is not their decision. And the experience of a son or daughter is not the same as the experience a parent might have had at the same age. When a parent is unsure, it's important to listen to the youth and what he or she has to say about faith. Keep in mind the developmental characteristics, and listen for answers appropriate to the age of the youth—not to the age of an adult. Honor the feelings and commitments of the young person. The youth have the right to judge their own readiness. Some may simply feel that they want to take longer to make a decision and want to attend confirmation class when it's offered again. Even within a single family, each member makes decisions in different ways. One may decide early to make a faith profession, while another might attend confirmation more than once before making a profession of faith. Each person must make the decision that is right for him or her.

> Keep in mind the development characteristics, and listen for answers appropriate to the age of the youth—not to the age of an adult. Honor the feelings and commitments of the young person.

## WHAT IF THE ANSWER IS YES?

What do we do when a young person decides to profess faith and join the church? We celebrate. This is a moment that we want the youth to remember all of his or her life. This is an important life decision. To profess Jesus Christ as Lord and Savior and to promise to live as a disciple of Jesus Christ is momentous enough that all who care for the youth want to stop, take notice, and celebrate. This

> **The celebration should include both the rituals and celebrations of the congregation and the rituals and celebrations of the family.**

celebration should include both the rituals and celebrations of the congregation and the rituals and celebrations of the family.

The celebration should include all who have participated in the confirmation experience: confirmands, parents, mentors, church leaders. You are actually celebrating two things:

- **The confirmation experience:** No matter what decision a person makes at the conclusion of the confirmation experience, the hope is that this time has been one of learning, friendship, deep sharing, and new relationships. Whether or not a youth joins the church at this time, the mentor, the family, and the congregation can celebrate this important time of learning we call confirmation.
- **The profession of faith and church membership:** This is an important faith step. The family, the mentor, and the congregation rejoices with the young people who make this decision.

## WAYS TO CELEBRATE

### MENTOR

- **Select a gift that will help the youth you have worked with remember the confirmation experience.** Consider writing a poem, or framing a photo of the youth participating in a confirmation session, or giving a gift to the church in honor of the youth, or giving a book of faith that has been meaningful for you.
- **Continue to pray for the youth.** The end of confirmation does not mean the end of caring for this young person.
- **Speak to your Sunday school class or covenant group** about why being a mentor has been a meaningful experience. Take time to let those who work with confirmation know about your experience as well.

* **Participate as invited** in celebrations planned by the family.
* **Make sure that you are present** for the worship service when the youth profess their faith.

## FAMILY

* **Ask about the congregation's celebrations for confirmation.** Plan your family celebrations so that your youth can participate in both the family times and the congregational events.

* **Take lots of photographs.** Although these ought not be taken during the service, do have your camera ready and take photos before and after worship.

* **Plan a family gathering for the day of the worship service.** Even if that won't work, do plan a family gathering time to celebrate your youth's confirmation. Eating together, letting your youth share learnings and experiences from confirmation, and listening to other family members tell of when they first professed their faith all add to the importance of the day.

> Plan a family gathering for the day of the worship service.... Eating together, letting your youth share, ... and listening to other family members ...all add to the importance of the day.

* **Invite the mentor to be a part of a family gathering** if your child has had a mentor as part of the confirmation experience.

* **Give a gift.** This doesn't have to be an elaborate or expensive gift. The purpose is to commemorate the occasion with some item that the young person can treasure and use to recall memories of his or her confirmation. Appropriate gifts include a cross for your youth to place in his or her room, a piece of jewelry, or a framed letter to your child that you have written, telling about your child and his or her decision about faith.

* **Prepare a confirmation memory book.** Include some of the things you have written in this guidebook. Use photographs taken during confirmation. Include mementoes of field trips and retreats. Ask family members to write notes that can be placed in the book.

## CONGREGATION

You might not be one of the persons responsible for the congregation celebrations, but you might choose to suggest one or more of these to the planners:

> **Hold a confirmation celebration dinner.** Include mentors, family members, and those who have completed confirmation classes. Issue certificates acknowledging the successful completion of this confirmation experience.

> **Ask others in the congregation to make gifts.** The United Methodist Women, United Methodist Men, or various adult Sunday school classes or small groups might do something special for each person in confirmation. They might choose to present these gifts as part of the confirmation worship service or as part of a reception at another time.

> **Involve the confirmation class in worship leadership.** These youth have spent weeks or even years studying about the church and reflecting on faith. They are ready to lead. Give them the opportunity to do so.

> **Put photographs of the individual class members and the class in the church newsletter.** During the weeks of preparation, your congregation's newsletter might feature a confirmand each week, including a photo, the confirmand's likes and dislikes, information about his or her school and other interests, and quotations from the confirmand being profiled.

> **Have a short reception after the worship service on confirmation Sunday.** This allows time for the congregation to offer congratulations but still gives time for family celebrations.

Whatever you do, remember that this is a celebration of a milestone in the faith lives of these young people. Take it seriously, and let them know how much they are loved.

# CHAPTER 6

# After Confirmation, What Next?

As a parent, you may come to the end of the confirmation experience and say, "Wow! That was exhausting. I need a rest." You may welcome the end of sessions, and of planning the family calendar around the activities of your son or daughter's confirmation commitments.

As a mentor, you may rightly feel ready to close out this experience and look to the next calling for your time and talents in your congregation.

At the same time, you might find yourself missing the sessions. While it's hard work to reflect on faith and its impact on your life, it is hoped that this has been a rich time for you and for the confirmand. It has given both of you permission to talk about things that often go unsaid regarding God, Jesus, the Holy Spirit, the church, and your faith.

But confirmation was never meant to be the ending of a faith journey. It's one milestone in a lifetime of living as a Christian.

## parental support after confirmation

*Parents of younger youth may do one or more of the following to support their son or daughter after confirmation:*

- **Require your youth to attend worship and faith-formation opportunities.**

Do you remember the information in Chapter 2 about youth and brain development? If so, you will remember that the frontal lobe of the brain is still developing. That means that the ability to make decisions is still under development. While your youth may see himself or herself as fully mature, he or she still needs the guidance of adults for making decisions and regulating behavior. It is not a bad thing to continue requiring your youth to attend church through middle school and high school.

**❧ Help your youth determine actions to live out the promises that he or she made at confirmation to support the church with prayers, presence, gifts, service, and witness.**

Many youth will participate with other family members in activities that help them live out these promises when they might otherwise find it difficult to do so on their own. They will find opportunities to live out these promises through your congregation's youth group. Again, participating with others may be easier than trying to find a way to live out these promises alone.

> **Participating with others may be easier than trying to find a way to live out these promises alone.**

**❧ Identify other milestones in your son or daughter's life that allow for a faith response.**

Think of those times ahead of you as your child grows: celebrating special birthdays, receiving a driver's license, graduating from middle school and high school, making a decision about college or a career. All of these events can be marked by a parent-child conversation about the place of faith in the decisions to be made. These can also be opportunities to create a family ritual to recognize the growth happening within your youth.

**❧ Support your youth with devotional material, books about faith, and study Bibles.**

This might not seem important, but we want all Christians to have continued study and growth. This means equipping young people with the right tools. Continuing a subscription to *Devo'Zine* beyond confirmation allows youth to have a devotional guide that addresses the questions and needs of youth. See whether your son or daughter found topics in confirmation that particularly interested him or her. Ask your church staff for appropriate books on such topics as church history, religions of the world, or Christian fiction.

**⤞ Identify current movies that might have implications for faith.**

While you may not necessarily view a particular movie at the same time your youth does, you can still have rich conversations about what a particular movie says about faith and life.

**⤞ Continue family devotion times beyond the time of confirmation.**

The rituals you may have begun during confirmation will continue to have meaning and enrich the family. Such rituals as lighting a candle to signify Christ's presence at mealtime remains meaningful beyond the confirmation experience.

These are just a few of the ways to continue the growth and faith formation deepened through confirmation. Most important, though, is to maintain an active interest in the life and faith journey of the young person you're accompanying through this process of growing up in the Christian faith.

## and what about you who are mentors?

*Assure the youth with whom you've been working that you will continue to pray for and support him or her even after confirmation has ended. You may decide to do one or more of the following:*

**⤞ With parent approval, continue to stay in contact with your confirmand through scheduled phone calls or messaging.**

Setting up a schedule of a simple check in with each other every three or four months will allow you to remain supportive.

**⤞ Stay informed about youth-sponsored activities.**

Lend your support to the youth you mentored, as he or she asks for congregational support for youth mission projects or other opportunities led by youth.

**⤞ Continue to pray for the youth you have mentored.**

Just as the family observes milestones as a young person grows and develops, you may add your congratulations, support, and prayers to those surrounding this young person.

**❯ Continue to speak to and engage in conversation the youth you have mentored.**

This may sound like a very small matter; but sometimes, following the end of an "official" duty, we act as though we no longer know the person we have worked with. Acting this way will contribute to a youth's perception that adults don't care about youth. Speak when you see each other. Ask the youth how things are going. Show continued interest in the youth's activities.

## CONCLUSION

Through confirmation, parents, mentors, and a variety of adult leaders have accompanied young persons through a significant time in their faith journeys. Remember that, through the church, we support and encourage one another to keep on the path to Christian perfection. We all continue to grow as Christians. May God's love guide us, and may we live so that the love of God we experience is shared with others.